A discourse on the English constitution, extracted from a late eminent writer, and applicable to the present times

William Stevens

Nabu Public Domain Reprints:

You are holding a reproduction of an original work published before 1923 that is in the public domain in the United States of America, and possibly other countries. You may freely copy and distribute this work as no entity (individual or corporate) has a copyright on the body of the work. This book may contain prior copyright references, and library stamps (as most of these works were scanned from library copies). These have been scanned and retained as part of the historical artifact.

This book may have occasional imperfections such as missing or blurred pages, poor pictures, errant marks, etc. that were either part of the original artifact, or were introduced by the scanning process. We believe this work is culturally important, and despite the imperfections, have elected to bring it back into print as part of our continuing commitment to the preservation of printed works worldwide. We appreciate your understanding of the imperfections in the preservation process, and hope you enjoy this valuable book.

A DISCOURSE

ON THE

ENGLISH CONSTITUTION;

EXTRACTED FROM

A LATE EMINENT WRITER,

AND

APPLICABLE TO THE PRESENT TIMES.

Χρη το αυτο Φθεγγεσθαι τον ρητορα και τον νομον.   *Æsch.*
Σεβειν δε τας κρατουντας, αρχαιος νομος.   *Eurip.*

LONDON,

Printed for G. ROBINSON, at N° 25, Pater-noster Row.
MDCCLXXVI.

9p
AC 911 .1776 S75

Want is this the
Stamp
Bill?

PREFACE.

THE Editor of the following Discourse on the English Constitution, having been witness, for some years past, to the many dangerous absurdities, which have been published in factious News-papers, to corrupt the good people of England, and answer the purposes of a party, who have been working secretly and openly, in every possible way, to throw things into confusion, and bring about a change of the government, thinks it high time that something should be offered, to shew the public how they are imposed upon, and to furnish them with a few rational

tional principles concerning the nature of civil power, the necessities of society, and the positive laws of their own country. Hence they will soon see, that no plan can be made sense of, except that doctrine of allegiance against which they have been taught to clamour; and that *resistance to civil government*, asserted on principle, is nothing but the extravagance and nonsense of designing writers, who want to be resisting every thing for their own private ends.

Suppose I desire to trip up a man's heels and pick his pocket; what can I do better, to keep up my own credit, and promote my own purposes, than publish it to the world, and get it believed, if possible, that the *common rights of humanity* give one man a title to trip up another man's heels? And if many are persuaded into the same notion, till we are either too strong or too cunning for opposition, then the property of the public is at our disposal; which is the thing we had in view.

When this principle operates in low life, and raises a gang of thieves and housebreakers, the principle itself, and the effects of it, are equally detestable. And it ought to be abhorred as much in other cases: for what is every regular government but a larger sort of house? What is the public revenue but the pocket of the state? And are there no thieves who want to be breaking into such an house, *while the family is asleep?* Are there not a larger sort of pickpockets, having the same appetites and principles with those of the common sort, who would plunder the state as freely as the others rifle a pocket? There is indeed this difference betwixt the two classes; that the

the ordinary thief has but little to say, while his brother of higher degree turns orator, and with false principles and infinuating speeches, renders his profession honourable and popular, till a nation is betrayed into its own ruin, and becomes a spectacle of misery to other states, who have been wise enough to provide better for their own security.

Every government ought to be upon its guard against such men, before they have intoxicated the lower order of the people with that enthusiastic notion of natural privilege against positive law, which leads directly to rebellion: and the people should be better informed in due time, lest their ignorance make them a prey to those who labour so industriously to deceive them. To wean them from that patriotic froth, with which they have been so long treated, we

must

must teach them how to examine things by the plain rules of common sense and positive law; and then they will see how they have been dancing after the unsubstantial delusions of oratory, and discover at last, that there is no liberty without law, no security without obedience.

I never met with any discourse, on the subject of allegiance, better calculated to open their eyes than the following, and therefore would recommend the serious consideration of it to all those who wish well to their country, especially at this time when so many wish ill to it. It was written by a gentleman eminently skilled in the English law, who had studied the constitution with integrity of mind, and has represented it with very great ability. That the government of England, or any part of it, is *not legally resistible*

ible with force, is the position he lays down; and he proves it by considering the people's allegiance pursuant to the positive law of the land, and the rights of the English monarchy, as they are by law expressly and undoubtedly established.

A DISCOURSE

A DISCOURSE ON THE ENGLISH CONSTITUTION.

IF it be a truth that laws (however originated) bind a people, the people of England are bound not to resist with force the King, or those commissioned by him, in any case, or upon any pretence whatsoever. This is to be alledged as a fundamental principle in arguing from positive law; and hence it flows, and is a known maxim of the English law, that the person of the sovereign is not punishable nor coercible by force; and in the practicable forms of proceeding, transgressions against this law are judged upon accusations after the form of high treason. This consequence of law, the maintainers of resistance scarce deny; for they seem to go off from, and surmount positive law, supposing a power, which they call the people, superior to all law, having it in their hands to reduce laws and law-makers all together; and so they think they argue upon sure grounds. But this eludes the hypothesis, which is, that the people are subject, and bound by the laws: for it is the same as saying that there is no law but in active force, which force is not constant; for sometimes one, and sometimes another division or faction of the people proves to be strongest; and then the laws, if there may be any, are changeable, and that, which men call right and wrong, is contingent, as a weather-cock that varies with the air: all which is ridiculous to affirm in discourse. But in a nation that hath established laws, all questions of right and wrong are referred to executive power,

in

(3)

in such methods of determination as the laws have prescribed; that is by regular process before competent judges, against whom there is no just exception.

But farther, nothing can justify resistance, but what will amount to a just and legal defence upon an indictment of high treason. If so, examine all the ordinary pretensions for resistance, and they will be found wanting. As first, the abuse of royal power. That will not do, for it is a rule of law, that *the King can do no wrong*, because all acts of the government against law are nullities; and such have no legal effect, and justify no commissioner or agent whatsoever. Then, next, immediate violence from the person of the king upon a subject, will also fail; for *se defendendo* is no legal plea in case of an inferior officer, much less in treason; for the law against compassing the death of the king, hath no exception. Then, as to personal defects or incapacities, be it in the highest degree, as madness, lunacy, infancy, or negligence, they afford no matter of defence in treason; for whatever the resisters say, the law says there can be no such thing: for if human infirmity in such cases may be alledged, designing people will ever pretend it, to serve the turn of their ambition. In a word, the law owns no mischief to a people in general or particular, so considerable as to be put into the scales against high treason. *Littleton*'s rule, *better a mischief than an inconvenience*, sounds oddly; but it hath this very meaning, and is very good law; and the reason is, there can be no law but contingent mischiefs to particulars may, and often do happen; but the consideration of them doth not disable a law that hath a general view. And whoever argues against a law, from a supposition of such mischiefs possible, argues against all law, and for anarchy and confusion. The law hath likewise another rule, which respects the same case;

[5]

case; which is *de minimis non curat lex*: and no contingent mischiefs to particular persons are regarded against the general convenience of a law, especially when government, common peace, and protection depends upon it.

These maxims of law are sufficient to answer all the popular reasonings of men, built upon the possibility of particular mischiefs. But all reasoning is out of doors, where there is positive law. None will deny the statute of treasons to be law, and in full force. And then there is a new ground upon which the case stands; so that if there were any former maxims, modifications, practices, or settlements of power contrary to that, call them covenants, contracts, fundamental principles, or whatever you please, they all sink into and are drowned in that, as latter laws, not consistent with, always repeal former. And it is well it is so; for there are evidences in history,

that

that before the making of that law, which the lawyers say is but declaratory of what the law was in truth before, there were great stretches, and even *læsa majestas* was construed treason. A farther use shall be made of this statute, which was a vast ease and safety to the people, in some reflections by and by; and in the mean time let it be observed, that it is not fair to alledge for answer, that it is not ingenuous to refer to actual process, or course of law, and the consequences of it; because all governments will take care of themselves, and that the laws shall be declared entirely on their side; as if this insisting on positive law were a subterfuge rather than an argument. But such answer cannot be allowed to be just, or any colour: for will not all irregular persons, as well as traytors, viz. felons, and other evil doers, if they may come off so, or if they are too strong for the judge, answer the same thing? why the one more than the other? To object power, againſt the force of poſitive law is ridiculous; for without a title to abſolute power, there can be no law at all. To temper this, therefore, in England, it is provided by law, that there be proper judges, competent to decide all queſtions of right and wrong, whether it concerns powers or intereſts, and ſuch as are put under all obligations of duty and oaths to do right according to law. But yet to enforce this reaſoning in favour of non-reſiſtance, and bring it to the height of demonſtration, let the judges immediate authority, though that be deciſive, be ſuſpended, and the caſe ſtated upon univerſal principles, and reaſons at large.

Now the terms, *non-reſiſtance* and *paſſive-obedience*, commonly uſed in this diſpute, are ſynonimous, and mean one and the ſame thing, that is, a negation of all active force, whatever the conſequence

quence be. *Obedience*, in the common acceptation of the word, founds active, and therefore doth not well bear such an adjective as *passive*; *non-resistance* is properly *passive*: but common use hath confounded the language, and diverse words or phrases brought to signify one and the same thing; which is only a choosing to suffer rather than obey unlawful commands. And it is very injurious to infer from such a behaviour, that any power or prerogative, more than is lawful is thereby recognized; but it is one way, and an effectual one, of flying in the face of an exorbitant power, and a flat contradiction to it. Thence it is inferred, that in all civil concerns, the law is the rule of obedience, whether *active* or (as it is termed) *passive*; only the former belongs to lawful, and the latter to unlawful commands. And there can be no better means of asserting the rights of the people by law, than the disowning unlawful commands by patient suffering.

'ing. For which reason the *passive obedience men* are the most express defenders of the laws against unbounded prerogative; as was demonstrated by the heroic carriage of some of the enthronised clergy towards the government in the last century.

And here it may not be amiss to observe, that instead of the old way of expression, the laws of this kingdom or nation, his Majesty's laws, the laws of the land, or the common law, some affect to use the word *constitution*; which in itself is no bad word, and means no other than as before. But it is commonly brought forward with a republican face, as if it meant somewhat excluding, or opposite to the monarchy, and carried an insinuation as of a co-ordination, or coercion of the monarchy: which latter term, viz. the monarchy of England, still implies, as of old, the whole law; as the crown, in all the authentic

thentic books is maintained to be *fons justitiæ*: and it is no where to be found that the crown was one thing, and the constitution another; but the true constitution of England is the monarchy as established by law. And so acts of parliament always refer (and anciently more express than now) to the grant and ordination of the crown, with the usual additions respecting the two houses. It is dangerous to vary the language of the law; because those, who do not well distinguish, are thereby carried into mistaken notions of the public.

As to precedents, they are not to be received as a rule of legal authority, but when done in quiet and regular times, approved and allowed by a constant usage in succeeding times: for escapes are no precedents. There have been some of this sort, witness the parricide of King Charles the First by Cromwell, who (to go no higher) died in his bed. Which action hath not been allowed a warrantable precedent; but yet wicked men, if permitted to have power, would alledge and use it as such. Undue precedents are very dangerous to liberty; for there are more and stronger instances of exorbitant prerogatives, than of republican encroachments; and the argument is as good for the one as the other. Therefore actions out of course, irregular, and time-serving, should not be received as precedents decisive, in justification of powers. These prejudices being removed, let the case of obedience be stated upon the true frame and oeconomy of right in the world, and particularly upon the general or common law of England.

In all governments that ever were or can be, the supreme power, wherever it is lodged, is and must be uncontroulable and irresistible. That is a truth included in the notion of authority or power,

power, for the one being granted, the other follows; as two and two are equal with four, becaufe, in the idea, they are one and the fame. Government refiftible is no government, and thofe, who fay the contrary, are to be talked with no more than fceptics in philofophy, who pretend to doubt every thing, even of their own effence, which that very doubting demonftrates. So that, in any fettled ftate, the fupreme power, whether it refides in one, a few, or many, may not be lawfully refifted, in any cafe whatfoever, by any coercive force.

In England, the fupreme authority is by law lodged in the crown, together with the two houfes of parliament, when duly affembled. It is not at all material whether, or how, it might have been otherwife placed; though it is naturally impoffible, that, in England, it can refide in all the people (as hath been vainly pretended to by fome *democratic* cities of of old) the people of England being separated too far asunder, ever to be immediately joined in one action. It is enough here, that, by indubitable law and right, the crown with the states of parliament, are to all intents the supreme authority, being what is termed the *legislative power*, which no subject ought to gainsay or resist. This will surely be granted; for whoever pretended to gainsay or resist an act of parliament, although, by natural possibility, it may be as iniquitous as any action of a single person can be? Lord Coke will have it, that acts of parliament, against common justice are void, as (for instance) if an act were past for erecting a judicature to determine *parte inauditâ alterâ*. But this must be understood in conscience and natural reason only, and not by the sentence of the courts of law; else, the acts to vest and divest private estates, and attainders of absentees, and divers others, would

would run a shrewd risk in Westminster-hall.

It necessarily happens, in the actual administration of government, that by reason the persons, invested with power, cannot act all things directly, the business is distributed in divers manners, according to the policy of several states, to answer the ends of government. As for the making, judging, and executing laws for punishing, defending, compelling, resisting, and the like. And these subdivided offices, or branches of power, may be committed to single persons, or bodies of men, as laws have provided; and then all those persons or authorities become parts of the supreme power in their respective provinces. And (without regard to wrong or right) as the whole supreme power is, so are they, in their proper jurisdictions, irresistible by law upon any pretence whatsoever; not allowing any man even liberty of self-pre-

preservation. For whoever thought it lawful for one accused, or condemned capitally, knowing himself to be innocent, and grosly abused in the judgment, to kill the judge or jury, or hang up the hangman to save his own neck? a man kills the bailiff that attacks him with force to take him; it is an offence capital, and he cannot plead *se defendendo*; and the law requires no proof of malice. These considerations reflect strongly upwards, upon the supreme power itself: for if the derivatives, in their offices, may not be resisted on any pretence, how comes the principal, or supreme in the execution of the whole power, to be resistible by force?

But farther, in England (whatever may be elsewhere) the grand distinction of the supreme power is into the legislative and the executive, which latter compriseth all actual coercion and force entirely in itself. As to the former, as the law now stands (for the opinions and modes of speaking, which took place in ancient times are dropt) it is most certain, that in real effect, the two houses of parliament have a co-authority with the crown in making laws; or it may be more agreeable, in other words, to say a negative voice upon all legislative acts; or a little more, that is, a sort of rogation, or power to move for, and give a spring to, new laws by petition, or otherwise, as the practice is. So as, in the main, no new law, of any sort, can be made or discharged for taxing, or otherwise, without the formal and actual concurrence of both houses of parliament; and either dissenting or non-consenting, no new law is or can be made. And this union of powers, in the making of laws, is that which, in England, is properly the supreme power absolutely and to all intents. The next thing is to consider how it is distributed, that is, between the crown and the two houses;

for

for there is no power or authority which is not derived from, or under, them or one of them.

And first, it is not found that the two houses, beyond this concurrent power in legislature, claim any proper agency whatsoever in the government. As for judicature in the lords house, it depends on the executive power of the crown, as other courts of justice do. Even private persons have often the like propriety in jurisdiction; and it is the king's justice, though administered by the lords: for the writs of error, that are the foundation of the legal jurisdiction, are returnable *coram rege in parliamento.* And, as to them and the commons, the office of counselling, petitioning, representing, &c. in virtue of the very words, excludes acting: and it is what every private person may, and often hath a right to do. But the houses, either severally or jointly, have this capacity in the highest degree,

gree, being the greatest council, and most universal representative that can be called or assembled legally in England. But yet, excepting the share in the legislative and judicature, no acts of the houses, or of either of them, are coercive, or will impeach any man at common law for disobedience; and as for matters of privilege, grown into course, the coercion is still (formally) granted by the crown, and an officer of the crown, the serjeant of the mace, assigned to execute the house's orders in matters of privilege. Else, the commons claim no judicature, not so much as power to administer an oath; and in matters of accusation, are petitioners to inform, as the sense of the word *impetitio* is, not unlike a grand inquest of the whole nation. All which matters are mentioned, left any of these particulars, if omitted, might be mistaken for an authoritative share in the executive government of England.

Then farther, it appears, that all the supreme power of the government of England, except only that which is lodged in the two houses of parliament, is to be found in the crown. The general inference from thence is plain and obvious; but to pursue it by steps. There are two conditions of the English government, the one in the sitting, and the other in the vacancy of parliament. The sitting, as to time, place, and continuance (saving the effect of the septennial act), is known to be in the pure direction of the crown; yet considering, that out of parliament, there may want means to petition or advise, *de arduis regni*, it is an act of conscientious trust and justice in the crown to the people in general (the said law apart), to hold frequent parliaments, and much more so according to that law, which turns it to a specific right, that the intent of it should be pursued. But, in all points whatsoever, saving what has been alledged, the government of England,

land, in and out of parliament, is exactly the same; and none can say, that the crown hath less power of government when the parliament is sitting than in vacation, nor more power in vacation than when sitting.

To obviate an objection, that, in vacancy of parliaments, there is no supreme power *in esse*, because no new laws can be made, without which capacity, the supreme power is imperfect, and, in the fullness of that authority, ceaseth; let it be observed, that a power of positive legislature is not incident to a supreme power, but it is often perfect without any legislative power at all. As in Turkey, according to the maxims of policy there, no power upon earth can alter their laws, for the laws result from the religion of the country; as here no power can alter the doctrines of the gospel. And, with them, the question is never what should be, but what is the law;

law; and yet there is a supreme power in the person of the emperor, as must be confessed. And the strains and abuses of ministers there, to serve the turns of power, and the pleasure of great men, against justice and their laws, is no answer to the constitution which, *in thesi,* is unalterable; and yet there is a supreme power. But to be more plain. If there were no laws at all in a country, but the will and pleasure of a potentate, or some juncto, were really and truly the law; that binds every subject in conscience to obedience. Yet even that supreme power is subject to rules, or law; for there is not, nor can there be, any power upon the face of the earth, above, or without law. For where none are declared, and there is no superior to exact accounts, yet the law of natural justice and equity prevail. And so a despotic ruler is tied up as much to the law, in duty and conscience, as any sub-governor is, who, by his commission, is restricted to rules. But this

duty

duty of all governments doth not impeach the notion of supreme, whether it be declared, or rests in the mind by nature. Either is without coercion, and equally obligatory. If coercion be supposed, then the power that coerceth takes the place of supreme: and it is a *Pelion* upon *Ossa* to set power over power; for that which hath the coercion of others, must be incoercible itself. And supposing that, and no obligation but conscience and duty in the supreme power, where is the difference, whether it be guided by positive and declared law, or by natural justice? All that can be said is, that laws assist the weak capacities of some men in power, by telling them what ought, and what ought not to be done, which their own natural skill might not perhaps have found out. Though I may say there is scarce a sincere person in the world, whom the golden rule, *do as you would be done by*, will not direct: so it is corrupt will, and not want of understanding, which often misleads men; and takes place against positive law, as well as against natural justice. So that it returns every way upon the conscience of powers; for if we admit a superior coercion, or in the common phrase, a liberty (with power) to resist, even that may be exercised with as bad a conscience as the other; and then what is got by the bargain?

But it is a most pernicious error to discharge the supreme power of the obligation to justice for conscience sake, as they do, who say acts of the supreme power, or (in the forensical style) legislative acts, or acts of parliament, are always just, and though made in partial cases, are not injurious because absolute. For a legislative or supreme power, wherever it resides, is as much bound to common justice and equity, in every public act, as a private man is obliged to common trust and honesty. And he that says such powers do no injury, though their act is (as in poſſibility it may be) moſt unjuſt and wicked, becauſe they cannot be contradicted, muſt, at the ſame time, allow that a private man who breaks a ſecret truſt, or kills his father, there being no evidence to check or convict him, is a very honeſt man, and hath done no wrong. Wherefore, if the conſciences of men were not ſome ſecurity in the general among promiſcuous ſocieties, and in the ordinary dealings of the world; the caſes of innocent men, who are moſt apt to rely on it, were very hard. But I dare ſay, that however open differences make a noiſe, there is in the world, as bad as it is, more juſtice among men, upon account of the common obligation of equity and conſcience, than from all the proceſs of law and coercion of the magiſtrate all the world over. And theſe men, who argue ſo ſtrongly againſt all truſt, eſpecially that lodged in governors, which is and will be a pure truſt as long as the world stands, only shew how little of that principle is to be found in themselves, which they think wholly wanting in others. It is most certain that numbers of men, whenever a public trust is reposed in them, may (I wish I could not as truly say sometimes do) break all the commandments of God, as well of the first as second table, as any private persons against whom they are chose to be a guard. And to conclude: the having power is so far from an excuse for doing bad things, that it aggravates them; as when dogs, that are to keep, worry the sheep. A common thief has more to say for himself, than an oppressor or murderer by power, who cannot be coerced. All these matters laid together make it plain, that whether there be a legislative power *in esse* or not, there is always a supreme power which commands all the forces of the state, and is by law, as well in the abfence as in the presence of the legislative, irresistible with force; and that will fall out to be the case of the crown of England.

These premises will most clearly appear, if we consider that the legislature, whereof the two houses partake, is of such a nature, that resistance with force doth not take place against it. For laws themselves are but the voice or words of power, and have authority to create a duty, but no active force to compel obedience, or to which resistance can be applied; for who can offer to resist a mere sound? When the executive power comes forward with a strong hand, then there is somewhat to resist, but not else. Therefore resistance or obedience, active or passive, relate wholly to the executive power, without which the legislative is weak and ineffectual. Now all the rest of the supreme power of the government

of

of England (except only legiflature, or the *non-refiftible* part, wherein only the two houfes are fharers) being owned to refide in the crown, it follows that the fame neceffity, which makes any power irrefiftible, makes the crown of England irrefiftible with force, upon any pretence whatfoever; which confequence is fo plain, that it need not be inforced with varying the expreffions, or with repetitions. And then upon the fame account, it follows that, as concerning the *paffive-obedience* or *non-refiftance* of the fubject with active force (legiflature always excepted, as not concerned in the queftion) the monarchy of England is the fupreme power, and ought not to be oppofed with force againft its force in any cafe, nor upon any pretence; fuch oppofition being a crime the laws ftyle treafon or rebellion; for which the fame laws allow no manner of juftification.

As to those nice arguers for resistance, who perpetually harp upon the abuse of power, and the sad effects of it, which they would prevent or cure by resistance, they are easily answered. The matter of right and wrong is indeed founded in nature, and in that quality, a law itself, however regularly enacted, may be (as before hinted) abominable and wicked: that is, the very legislative power, were it the majority of the people (which is not possible), or in select hands, as it ordinarily is, may tyrannize, and offend against all the rules of natural justice, common sense, and equity; for which that power is to answer, as having transgressed and broke their trust: but it is to God only; for else the correctors of them become at that instant the legislative power, and then we are where we were before. Now there is a distinction to be made here, which is between *misfortune* and *injury*. For if a subject is a sufferer

under

under a general, however wicked, law, he is unfortunate, but not injured; becauſe he can claim no more than the common benefit of the laws of his country. And having, in due form, ſtood the judgment of the law, he can aſk no more; his appeal muſt be above; there is no power on earth to relieve him. This was the caſe of Socrates, and we have his example, as well as reaſonings, in the report of his caſe, to confirm what is here maintained. In ſhort, it is abſolutely impoſſible ſo to order affairs, but that whoever hath power to do right, hath of conſequence, power to do wrong. And if reſiſtance be introduced upon a ſuppoſal (which may be made no leſs arbitrarily and inſincerely than any act of power can be, and commonly is ſo) of the undue and inſincere uſe of regular powers, it is declaring plainly, that there can be no government nor diſtributive juſtice at all in the world.

And

And to complete the argument, the positive law, or statute (which was mentioned before, but not specified as to one article) is absolutely decisive of the question, in the very terms. It is the article in the statute of 25 Edward III. which makes it high treason to levy war. This is an expression so general, that it forbids resistance upon any pretence; for the government is armed, and if opposed at all, must be opposed by arms, that is in array of war, or (as they say) *more guerrino*. And whatever the cause is, tho' not directed, perhaps, against the King, but to pull down bad houses, destroy engine looms, and the like popular, and (as they think) meritorious purposes, it is solemnly adjudged to be treason, as levying war within this article. So that resistance with force, which must be by levying war, is prohibited on pain of death by a positive law; which puts the matter past all dipute.

As to the objection, that *passive obedience* or *non-resistance* is a slavish and degenerate principle, it is a mistake; so far from it, it is a principle of liberty and security. For can any man be free, and safe from the outrages of oppressive, potent neighbours, who doth not live under a power sufficient to keep the peace, and protect him? The sovereign power is high and remote, and commonly the interest of it is to be a friend to the *community*. If the abuses, when there are any, fall hard upon the great men who are near it, they are compensated in the share that devolves among them; with which they would be more ready to oppress their inferiors, if somebody were not above them to give protection and redress. And if the lusts and disorders, sometimes incident to power, bring evil upon the people, it is scarce ever so great, but they are amply compensated by the ordinary peace and protection they enjoy.
There

There is much more danger of oppreſſion to a common man from bad neighbours, private enemies, and wrong doers,
as alſo from the cabals at the next door,
than from the potency of the government, though it ſhould happen to be
none of the beſt. And it is found that
the worſt governments are thoſe that have
moſt heads and hands; for the abuſes of
ſuch are more diffuſed, and turn to a
more general oppreſſion.

In regard to the queſtions put by ſome
men—As, can it be imagined a nation
ever ſubmitted to be tyrannized over by
one man? Or is it fit that one man
ſhould have it in his power to make all
the reſt miſerable? However impertinent
theſe queſtions are to the cauſe, in a juſt
way of reaſoning, yet they may be an-
ſwered by other queſtions. As, can it
be believed, that a people were ever
willing, or conſented, that thieves, ma-
lefactors,

lefactors, and cheats, every where in plenty, should have liberty to ravage and destroy at their pleasure? And will not a people choose rather to be subject to one man's pleasure, upon a fair understanding, who is potent and can protect them, than be left at large to fight it out continually, in clans and combinations to gain a little defence and safety? They must answer, if any thing, right: but then, say they, you may change, and have a better government. True, you may change, but seldom comes a better. If they say it is better the government be weak and precarious, because, for fear of themselves they will do no injury. No, nor yet (through the same fear) hinder others from doing injury, which is worst of all; and who lives that has not had experience of this? But not to refine farther, let it be only observed, that the force of the argument of the resisters lies in magnifying the evils of bad government, and they will have those evils taken in the utmost extremity, though but

but naturally possible, and in no sort probable, if ever known to have happened in the world. But they say nothing of the evils that attend the want of power in a government, which make a sharper catalogue by much than the other; and they are such as never fail to happen, and, what is worse, affect the whole people wherever they do happen; as all must know by experience, when the nerves of government have been relaxed. No political state is perfect, and the least evil is the best. Public good, so much in these men's mouths, is a cloak which hypocrites always wear, and if you turn it up a little, the nasty self-interest, injustice, and oppression will appear, that lie lurking under it. Those, who have been more than once burnt, which is the case of the English nation, will (it is to be hoped) watch well such fuel. The hardest case of the justest government is, that they are forced to deceive to make people happy; that is, to be quiet, or to take what is good for them. Give me me the private man that dares be honeſt, and the government that dares do juſtice. Men who live in peace and ſafety, which are the ordinary fruits of government, are like men in health; then they are not contented, but long for preferment, honour, luxury, and pleaſures: but when they fall under diſeaſes, and are in pain, then they would quit all for pure health and eaſe.

It is not foreign to theſe ſpeculations, to put in a word in behalf of the Engliſh monarchy and government, which hath many advantages to the people, but none more glorious than this; *that all acts of the crown, againſt law, are mere nullities*; and all, who act under them, are obnoxious to the law, and ſo far from being protected, that they may be queſtioned and puniſhed by that very power, againſt whom its own command is no defence or juſtification. And for this cauſe, all authentic commands are put in writing,

writing, or sealed, or no person, served with such command, can be prosecuted for contempt in not obeying. For the party may know by that, whether it be a legal command, which requires active obedience, or not; and then by whose fault it is sent forth, whereby the proper officer may be brought to answer for it. This constitution never was heard of in any state but the English, nor is it extant in force under any other government upon earth: so little danger is there of excesses from the English monarchy. But if I were debarred this patriarchal privilege, and had my lot in times of disorder, and were put upon a choice of the two, I would certainly, upon the competition, rather yield to one absolute potentate, *tale quale,* who had power sufficient to govern and protect, than to live in perpetual fear and proper guard against injury and oppression from the most cruel of all sorts, that is (not superiors so much as) equals, or rather inferiors. It is an

observ-

observation, which the general experience of ages may vouch, *viz.* that the calamities, which have fallen upon the people of England from the state of the government, have been incomparably more by reason of too little, than of too much power exercised by the kings; and that by how much nearer the state hath warped towards what some call a commonwealth, by so much hath tyranny got ground, and the true liberty of the people sunk down; whereof great part never emerged to them, no not after the former government hath been happily restored.

But to conclude with doing right to the cause, I must needs say, that it is not a just balance of interest which always regulates the good or evil consequences of power; but the mere shew, name, opinion, and prejudice, or rather humour of the people go a great way in it. For it may be observed, that it is not enough to do men good, but they must think

think and accept of it as such, and also trust their government; or else, whatever the truth is, they will not flourish in numbers and increase of trade and wealth. Therefore it is a most wicked practice of the faction, to labour, as they do, to create misunderstandings and distrust in the people of their government, which must needs tend to the destruction of their welfare and increase. Now, to consider the case rightly, and make a judgment from the extremes, it is almost impossible, that prosperity, by increase of people and wealth, should happen under the great *Asiatic* monarchies (although now, as the world transcends in wickedness, there can be no other than absolute government there); for the people cannot have reason to think themselves safe and secure in the advances they make, and, being careless of that, are ambitious of nothing but power to tyrannize over others, as they themselves are tyrannized over by their superiors; they think of no

pros-

prosperity but through oppression; and so, by common consent, all are slaves. And this wolvish humour is such, that the governments think their security lies in the destruction and depopulation of provinces. And, to say truth, all defection from common honesty and truth, which should tie people reasonably together, not only tends to, but makes absolute government necessary. Hence, from the very name of monarchy, men derive a prejudice, as if no security for life or estate were had under it; when it may be made appear, that in monarchic countries, which have laws of government, as well as of property, such as we call mixt, there is more real security than is to be found elsewhere, although there may be much more pretension to it. To instance in the pretended republics of Venice and Holland; the former is a pestilent aristocracy of the worst sort, that is, of a multitude, under which the community of the people have no law or justice

tice on their side, but as they gain the protection of one great man against another. And the other is Holland, which hath no popular elections (essential to a republic), but burgomasters fill vacancies by a majority of themselves; and so a faction is always prevalent, both in the towns of which the combination consists, and in the stadthouse, whereby the lands of the countries all about are made direct slavish, and sometimes taxed so as not be worth owning; and all to save the citizens purses; and all preferments and succession run in a match-making channel and family relation; and yet the name of republics holds these in credit, and the people are pleased, increase and thrive. But whatever becomes of the humour and fancies of people, it is certain, that for the true utility of government, when sedition is not permitted to grow too much upon it, the government of England is the safest and best government in the world.

F I N I S.

CPSIA information can be obtained at www.ICGtesting.com
Printed in the USA
LVOW022245301112
309553LV00014B/662/P